D1107483

Books from the **Attic**
4100 Bonita Road
Bonita, CA 91902
(619) 479-2333

2 30
UH6

DORIS W. S. Stowe
1100 Boulder Road

PHYLLIS DILLER'S marriage manual

PHYLLIS DILLER'S marriage manual

Drawings by Susan Perl

DOUBLEDAY AND COMPANY, INC.
GARDEN CITY, NEW YORK

Copyright © 1967 by Phyllis Diller
Library of Congress Catalog Card No. 67-25594
Designed by David Miller
Manufactured in the United States of America

Publishing Consultant: J. P. Tarcher, Inc.

Dedicated to my darling

husband, Warde Donovan,

the Richard Burton of the

Geritol set.

Table of Contents

Foreword

Do you have a marriage that is constantly in the repair shop? Do you have the feeling even Maury Wills wouldn't steal home if it was like yours? Was the last time you smiled for your wedding photograph?

Since marriage is a private institution and not supported by public funds, I want to help.

You may think you know all the rules you need to—like "No rabbit punches" and "No kidney blows"—but I have some other suggestions that will make "Till death do us part" seem like not quite so long.

First and foremost, get married with the feeling it is going to last. Not like the bride I knew who doubled the wedding cake recipe and froze one.

Sometimes I think brides and wives have a tendency to forget husbands are people. While we all know that happiness in marriage depends on how well the husband minds, there are subtle, underhanded methods of getting across to him the fact that the Wedding Bell is *not* the Liberty Bell.

Many marriage experts say, "Live in the present. Don't anticipate what might happen." I cannot go along with this. If you have a marriage like mine, you'll be happier worrying about the future.

This book deals with reality and teaches the kinds of truths not available in other so-called marriage manuals.

Chapter I — *I Met Him Through a Broken IBM Machine* — explores the terrible problem of knowing what kind of man you have chosen. This information can save you from making the awful mistake I made.

When we married, Fang was so far over the hill he got more excited over a filled prescription than a filled sweater. Really it's too much when your husband insists that you toast his Zwieback.

Chapter II — *Misery Loves Company* — contains intimate romance and sex instructions.

Remember beauty isn't everything and sometimes the most handsome men make the worst husbands, and vice versa. One of my friends who is happily married has a husband so ugly she met him when a friend sent him over to her house to cure her hiccoughs.

Whatever you may look like, it's wise to marry a man your own age. As your beauty fades, so will his eyesight.

Chapter III—*Marriage On the Rocks*—deals with the maintenance of domestic tranquility. You will learn that the proper thing to say if your husband comes in unexpectedly, while you're describing him to the kids, is "... and experts agree stupid, lazy drunken men make the best fathers."

You will also learn that you shouldn't be one of those women whose husbands outgrow them. Read a lot. Take courses at night school. I have a friend who can say, "Shut up, ya bum," in seven languages.

This chapter also warns against trying to interpret everything your husband says because you may miss some wonderful insults that way. An example of this was when Fang said, "I'll take some of that fab gravy."

I thought he meant fabulous—weeks later he told me he meant it tasted like soap.

Let me tell you, a discussion that starts, "I'll tell you something you do that irritates me, if you tell me something I do that bothers you," never ends in a hug and a kiss.

Chapter IV — *The Power Behind the Thrown* — instructs on the nature of man — laziness. It offers the consolation that unless you're married to a Henry VIII you're more than likely to outlive your husband. Your husband realizes this and by being lazy he may be thoughtfully preparing you for widowhood.

Of course, Fang isn't lazy, he's just professionally unemployed. I don't mean to say Fang changes jobs, but he could have been on What's My Line? every week since the program started. If your husband gets fired as often as Fang, I will pass on this important tip. When he calls and says he's bringing the boss home to dinner, don't start getting it ready until 5:30.

Chapter V —*My Mother-In-Law Wears Army Shoes* — reveals how to live with the disgusting fact that, as a group, mothers-in-law are the longest-lived obsolete species in the world.

Chapter VI — *His Car Has More Insurance Than I Do* — teaches how to call a bail bondsman, explain why the rear bumper is in the back seat, and what not to say to a wise-guy policeman.

In the Appendixes at the back of the book I have

tried to deal with certain unexplored aspects of wedding etiquette, such as:

1. Before you get married you should meet your fiancé's parents. It is not enough that you like his parole officer.

2. When the bridal consultant says you should have traditional wedding music, it does not necessarily mean what has been played at your four previous weddings.

3. When in a wedding line, don't say to the bride and groom, "I just hope you'll be as happy as we thought we'd be."

Finally, I have provided a happy marriage test which is certain to clear up any remaining problems.

Perhaps the greatest lesson I've learned is that *SELF-PITY IS BETTER THAN NONE.* This being the case, is it any wonder I decided to write a Marriage Manual?

PHYLLIS DILLER

CHAPTER I

I Met Him
Through A Broken
IBM Machine

It might help you to be more satisfied with your mate if you remember that when you made the selection it was not multiple choice. I was sort of tricked into marrying. One night I was out with Fang and a girl said, "You better hang on to him." I thought I had a prize. I didn't know she meant that after one drink he falls down.

I always wondered how I could tell when the right one came along—but it was easy. He was the only one that came along.

Unfortunately, there is no way of looking up husbands in Consumer's Guide. For instance, Fang told me he was a self-made man. It wasn't until later that I discovered that he would have been wise to get some help. With him there's no question that it would have been better to have loved and lost. So that you know what kind of a man you have on your hands—they're so clumsy, they'll stand anywhere—I have listed a few tell-tale characteristics.

Baby Man

I knew something was wrong when Fang asked the dentist for the tooth he pulled so he could put it under his pillow. Once when I told a woman to leave Fang alone, she said she wasn't trying to seduce him, she was considering adoption. Your husband is immature if...

1. He asks for a balloon when he buys a pair of shoes.

2. He doesn't object to your smoking so long as you let *him* blow out the match.

3. At quitting time he asks the boss to help him put on his boots.

4. When you go to bed at night, the books he brings with him are to color.

5. The reason he behaves at the office Christmas party is because he believes Santa is watching him.

6. When you're gone for a week, he greets you with "What'd you bring me?"

In Sickness And In Sickness

Some people get walking pneumonia. Fang gets lying-down hangnails. When the doctor says, "There's nothing wrong with you" he says, "Look again, Doctor, my X-Rays always flatter me." Incidentally, when Fang gets a low prescription number, he believes it means the doctor thinks he's important. Your husband is a hypochondriac if . . .

1. He puts *cough syrup* on his pancakes.

2. Instead of an olive in his martini, he has a Tum.

3. He heats his band-aids.

4. He wears a cummerbund just to hold a hot water bottle.

5. The reason he notices you is because you are wearing a pillbox hat.

6. He has a thermometer attached to his watch chain.

7. He's still wearing his hospital identification bracelet over a year after he's left the hospital.

8. He not only lists his medical expenses on his tax form but insists on putting down every diagnosis.

Of course, if *you* get ill, expect something from him like, "The steam from the dishwasher will make you feel better," or "Keep scrubbing. The air is always cleaner near the floor."

Cheap Isn't The Word For Him

Fang is such a tightwad that when we go out at night, he has the kids put on a song and dance act and charges the baby sitter a cover charge. Instead of buying us an electric blanket, he got himself a pair of electric pajamas. Your husband is a tightwad if . . .

1. Your car insurance policy is $10,000 deductible.

2. Instead of taking you on vacations, he hangs 50 state pennants in the living room.

3. Instead of getting tickets when you go out, you're always going to places where you get your hand stamped.

4. When you turn the heat up over 60, he accuses you of arson.

5. When you ask him for spending money he replies, "I gave at the office."

A Young Man On His Way Down

When I met Fang the earth stood still. The earth started up again, but he stood still and never did get going.

I'll tell you, it's no fun having a husband up on blocks. I remember once a vocational director said to Fang, "You must develop some mechanical skills—like getting out of bed."

Everybody knows how much time Fang spends in bed. A local store that gives a 30 days' trial on mattresses gives Fang only 15 days. Your husband is lazy if...

1. When he leaves the house, he finds out which way the wind is blowing and goes that direction.

2. His idea of dressing for dinner is wearing a necktie over his pajamas.

3. The family bulletin board lists his sleeping schedule. He schedules make-up naps.

4. He listens to the weather on the Today Show and won't go to work if it's raining any place in the country.

5. The directions on his medicine say, "A teaspoon before going to bed," and in one day he uses seven bottles.

6. After his vacation, instead of a suntan he has bedsores.

7. Coffee doesn't keep him awake—even when it's hot and being spilled on him.

The only way I can get him up in the morning is to have a tootsie roll waiting for him when he walks across the room to turn off the alarm.

When His Cup Runneth Over,
He Licks It Off The Bar

Fang never stops drinking. When we go out and he can't finish his tenth drink, he pours it into a doggie bag. Your husband drinks too much if . . .

1. He rings in every new day.

2. When he takes you out under the stars to make love, he sees the Big Dipper and it makes him thirsty.

3. He makes arrangements to meet you in Grand Central Station *on top* of the clock.

4. He starts a whiskey chain letter.

5. Bottles outnumber the cans two to one in your disaster supply.

6. He says he never drinks alone, but considers the goldfish somebody.

And For My Next Trick

I have the only husband who's such a show-off that he does the Watusi to Star Dust. Your husband is a show-off if . . .

1. Someone is singing the Lord's Prayer and he says he knows all five verses.

2. He goes to a Chinese restaurant and orders a pizza.

3. He gets the beer concession at a WCTU convention.

4. He reports more than he actually makes on his income tax.

5. He does his push-ups on the subway.

The Little Man Who Wasn't All There

They say marriage is a two-way street, but mine is only one-way, and I have the feeling I'm going the wrong way on it.

I began to suspect Fang wasn't so smart when I discovered it was necessary to paste pictures on our grocery list. He must have a Teflon brain — nothing sticks to it.

Once you have one, husbands are not easy to get rid of but here are a few tricks you might try.

1. Remember—no matter how well you wrap him, Goodwill Industries does not take husbands.

2. Get a brown tweed davenport the same material as his brown tweed suit. This will make it much easier to ignore him.

3. Take the ID cards out of his billfold so if he ever gets amnesia he won't be returned to you.

4. Send him out for a bottle of milk. By the time he gets back you can move.

Marry In Haste—Repent At Leisure

Of course I should have known I wasn't marrying well when my folks gave me a *de*nouncement party.

Some wives have model husbands, I got one that needed remodeling.

Still, no matter how far your mate comes from living up to your expectations:

1. Do not refer to him as a husbandette.

2. If your husband wants to lick the beaters on the mixer, shut them off before you give them to him.

3. When your husband tells you how good you've got it, don't say, "Yeah, compared to life in India."

4. If you're late getting ready, as you come out don't say, "Better late than never." He's apt to say, "Not necessarily."

5. Remember there is no way you can give the father custody of the children without getting a divorce.

CHAPTER II

Misery

Loves

Company

June, Moon And Goon

In writing this book I have tried to give a proportionate amount of space to these aspects of marriage which I knew about from my personal experience. Unfortunately, sex is barely mentioned.

All Fang knew about sex when we married was what he had learned in the Boy Scouts—and what good was that to me?

If it's too late for your husband to get sex education in the classroom, let him know that he can still pick up some information at the poolroom.

For all my suffering I did learn one cardinal rule which I can pass on to you. *NEVER REFER TO YOUR WEDDING NIGHT AS THE ORIGINAL AMATEUR HOUR.*

Out Of Sight—Out Of Your Head

I don't care how happily married you think you are, remember it's up to you to make your husband stay with you. Don't be a square in a triangle.

Once I was telling a friend, "Fang admits he is insanely jealous of me." Fang spoke up and corrected me, "What I said was 'If I were jealous of you I'd be insane.' "

Actually there's no need to be suspicious about your mate. You'll always know if anything is going on. People pretend they don't want to tell you, but they're all dying to. I had a friend who was raving about her husband and said, "You know he's too good to be true," and three people said, "Oh, you've heard."

1. Every so often check to see if he's digging an escape tunnel under the house.

2. Don't bother checking up on your husband while he's at work. You won't catch him at anything anyhow unless you can parachute onto the skylight of his office, in which case you will break your leg like I did.

3. Unfortunately an ordinary fence around the yard
   will not keep a husband from wandering. I've got
   mine electrified.

But if you enjoy being jealous, go ahead, and here's
some help:

1. Ask him how much he tipped for lunch. This will let
   you know if he bought one or two lunches.

2. On a night he's going out, give your teen-age son the
   family car. Your husband will have to take the one

with the souped-up motor, and it will be a simple matter to know when he comes in.

3. No matter how gray you get his handkerchief don't let him use Kleenex. Of course, if she is very young she'll wear white lipstick and handkerchief checking won't help.

4. If you can still smell Spearmint in the gum, he's had a drink on the way home.

Advice To The Love Worn

From observing the couple next door, I can tell you there *is* such a thing as too much togetherness.

When they moved in, you couldn't believe how icky-sticky they were—my binoculars would steam up. Last week, a year later, their marriage counselor was given permission to use a siren on his car.

Here are a few of their little together acts I would suggest not bothering with:

1. Do not use the same section of a revolving door.

2. Do not climb under the curtain so you can be in the same voting booth.

3. If he picks up the receiver to make a call, let him dial the number.

4. When you play checkers do not sit on the same side of the board.

Fang and I tried togetherness. We got matching swim suits, but Fang broke the strap on his.

How To Make Your Husband Less Amorous

Every night when we go to bed, Fang proves that it's not true that the worst time for most marriages is the waking hours. He is the kind of husband who talks me into making love by saying, "Read your contract," so I have devised a few simple rules to keep him calm:

1. Try saying, "Good night, Chet," and if he is sleepy he may say, "Good night, David," and turn over.

2. Give him a lot of chores to do in the evening, or keep him out late so he is exhausted when he gets to bed. This tactic might be known as "Poop Art."

3. If you look like I do, merely leave the light on till he goes to sleep.

4. Remember—the command "stay" seldom works.

What Ever Happened To Love?

Remarks of Men That Come to a Screeching Halt
One Minute after the Ceremony:

1. "You look beautiful when you're mad."

2. "Eat up . . . you don't have to worry about that figure."

3. "I guess you know you can wrap me around your little finger."

4. "Who wants to go out with the boys when I can be with you?"

5. "I don't care who sees me kiss you."

6. "You look pale. Remember, you shouldn't overdo."

7. "Watch a football game when I can walk down the street and show you off?"

8. "Don't keep anything to yourself. When you're bothered about something, speak up."

9. "Nothing is too good for *you!*"

How To Earn A Loving

To maintain the romance in your marriage you should fix yourself up in the morning. It's only fair to your husband. One morning I tripped and fell into the trash barrel and Fang had to go to the City Dump to bail me out.

Once I suggested that Fang call me "Baby." He refused. He said, "Listen, every time I've called you that, we've had one."

1. Baby doll pajamas are romantic attire. Wear them even if you do have to buy them in size 52.

2. Launder the sheets. The shock of having clean and ironed sheets will keep him awake for a few minutes anyway.

3. Turn down the heat in the bedroom at night. It's more fun to be do-it-yourselfers.

CHAPTER III

Marriage On The Rocks

A Love Match—15 Rounds

Everyone loves a lover, and even more a couple having marital trouble. Even though you realize how happy it would make others, don't let anyone know how you really get along. Say things like—"We just marked our tenth wedding anniversary." Don't add, "We marked it with a circle on the calendar and threw darts at it."

I realize it is normal to argue. I almost missed World War II watching my parents fight. The only thing they had in common was 15 kids.

Early in our marriage Fang and I agreed not to keep petty annoyances like the top off the toothpaste, crackers in bed, to ourselves. We have always shouted things over.

It's nice to be a Pollyanna, but of course use a little discretion in this. Not like the woman whose husband came home, told her he had been fired and she cheerfully said, "Oh well, it'll be something to put in the Christmas letter."

Even if you were captain of your high school debating team all seven years, it is still necessary to learn how to win an argument with a husband. Unless you achieve finesse in winning your point your home could be in a constant state of civil war. And it isn't easy to have the militia called out to your home.

No Exit

There is no Geneva Convention in home arguments.

Remember all is fair in war and war. To properly condition a husband it is important that he feel trapped. Never let him off the hook.

1. When he comes down for breakfast, ask him, "Well, how do you want your arguments this morning?"

2. When you play cards, insist that queens are higher than kings.

3. Sign your Christmas cards Mrs. and Mr.

4. Get a tape recording of you nagging for your husband to play when you're out of town and he gets lonesome.

While You're Up, Call The Marriage Counselor

It's amazing people get married at all. Other things you get that you plan to keep a lifetime come with a guarantee. When you pick a mate all you get is "in sickness and in health," "for richer or for poorer." Scare clauses.

But actually couples are not advised to be cautious enough. The weather bureau sends out warnings of impending tornadoes but there is no such service that predicts the storms in marriages. I have therefore compiled a list of some marital danger signals:

1. If during the wedding ceremony he leans over and whispers, "I feel like there is something important I should be doing."

2. He has his little black book Xeroxed so he can have a copy in every suit.

3. If you have more than 52 arguments a year and each one lasts at least a week.

4. He writes a letter to the editor urging that the Government draft married men with children first.

5. He starts wearing a prisoner of war shirt around the house.

6. He borrowed money from the bank to send you on a vacation and called it a Home Improvement Loan.

Here are a few responses to such provocation:

1. When you make out the family budget envelopes for rent, food, insurance, etc. be sure there's one clearly labeled "Divorce."

2. Replace the blue ribbon on your old love letters with a black one.

3. Take your wedding ring box with you whenever you leave the house.

4. Go to the Post Office and ask for a different zip code than your husband.

5. If in a weak moment he asks, "Do you love me?" reply, "Well, let me think about it."

6. On your anniversary, hire someone to come to the house to play Taps.

The Best Defense

Try to put your husband in the wrong no matter what the situation. For example:

1. If he walks in when you're in the arms of another man, quickly say, "That's right, always put me on the defensive."

2. If he ever really gets furious and starts a fight when you are not ready for one, put it off by saying, "Darling, I love the way you look when you're angry."

3. When he has a good point and you want to make him forget it—(a) grab your heart, (b) moan softly, (c) sink slowly to the floor. If he comes over to you, whisper, "I'll be all right, dear, what were you saying?" If he repeats it, ask for a divorce.

4. Don't forget—you can't win today's fights with yesterday's arguments. Say modern-sounding things like, "If you don't change your ways I'm going on LSD."

You Can't Win 'Em All

Don't ever bring up an old argument that you won. He might very well come out with all the things he "should have said." Remember it isn't like a TV rerun. The next time he might accidentally be the victor.

You should not insist on coming out ahead in every fight. It's a lot more interesting for the kids to watch a fight if they aren't absolutely sure which side is going to win.

It's all right to lose, as long as you *don't* do it gracefully. After an argument come home and say:

1. "Harold, my psychiatrist, says I'm being too permissive with you."

2. "All the girls at the luncheon agreed with me."

3. "All right, that's your decision for 1967."

When he complains you're browbeating him, ask him if he wants to be different from other husbands.

King For A Second

Although it never happened to us, some couples may get argued out. To reignite the fires, try the following:

1. He tells you about what his Lodge has planned for Ladies' Night, and you say, "Funsy, funsy!"

2. Accuse him of squandering his paycheck on rent, insurance and fuel oil.

3. Say, "Why don't you get your check cashed on the way home? Just down the street there's a Koolade stand."

4. When he offers to give you a kiss, say, "I've already had one."

Nine Rules Of Household Warfare

1. Do not refer to your wedding day as your inauguration day.

2. Do not quarrel in front of guests. Husband and wife fights should never be invitational sporting events.

3. Remember—never go to bed mad. Fang and I never did. However, one year we were up for nine months. Caution: I know a woman who ignored this advice. She's now the mother of 15 children.

4. Try to remember to say "please" when you tell him to "shut up."

5. It's all right to nag, nag, nag, but it is not right to bawl him out for giving you laryngitis.

6. Teach him to fight fair during arguments. I hate nasty little things like when Fang says, "Well, then, it's just my word against your 2,000."

7. If you're divorced and remarried don't be constantly belittling your ex-husband. Concentrate on the present one.

8. When you take separate planes say it is for the sake of the children, not because you can't stand him.

9. You aren't communicating well enough if you argue for two hours and suddenly find you're on the same side.

Typical Arguments And How To Win Them

Fang and I learned to fight about everything. We even had fights about which family to spend Christmas with. Neither of them wanted us.

Here are several typical arguments and how to win them:

A. If he's caught you using his razor, and unless you want a Madison Square bathroom, take care of it in one of the following ways:

1. Tell him you were trying to decide whether or not to get him a new one.

2. If it happens to be a new one, tell him you were making up your mind whether it should be exchanged.

3. If it was a gift from his mother and can't be exchanged, explain you wanted to know how good a razor it was so you'd know how much to spend on her.

(The above is for an electric razor. If it's a straight edge he catches you with, he'll be afraid to voice an objection.)

B. Men are forever harping on putting money in a savings account. While you realize you haven't got enough put away for a rainy day to buy a cheap umbrella, you know you don't want to start scrimping now, so you'd better have a few arguments ready. Try starting the discussion with . . .

1. "Remember March 6, 1933 when the banks closed? They say something like that happens every 35 years."

2. "They're always lending money to people I can't stand."

3. "I suppose you'd like me to balance a bank book on my head in church on Sunday morning instead of wearing a new hat?"

4. "How much do you think the pioneers had in the bank?"

5. "I don't believe in banks—stores."

C. You want a new fur coat, and you know it won't help one bit to threaten holding your breath till you're blue in the face because that's your natural color. Here are a few other suggestions:

1. Every time you go outside in your cloth coat, cough.

2. Tell him you're gaining weight and larger size mink coats cost more.

3. Tell him you saw a mink coat that you like that costs only $35 tax, plus the price.

4. Explain that it will look like he got a raise.

5. Start sewing mouse skins together on the dining-room table.

A Man's Home Is His Wife's Castle

Most husbands have feet of clay and track them all over the house.

Husbands aren't comfortable when they have wives like my neighbor, Mrs. Clean. Why, she is so neat she catalogues her wastebasket! After she shampoos her rug, she makes her husband walk around the edges of it for a month. Imagine not being able to jay-walk in your own living room!

If he ever tries to argue with you about your housekeeping . . .

1. Explain to him the house is in exceptionally good condition, considering you only clean during commercials.

2. About once a month say, "Today I'm going to let everything go and do such and such." That gives the *impression* you don't let everything go every day.

3. Tell him that Mrs. Clean's husband was oiling his gun and accidentally shot himself in the head. She mopped the rug before she called the doctor.

Never Give A Sucker An Even Break

Your husband should never have a good time if you're not there to ruin it for him. If he's going off without you, here are a few remarks and ideas which may keep him at home.

Golf

1. As he goes out the door, say, "Don't feel guilty about leaving me with all these kids. I'll try to make a game of it—five fights an hour can be par."

2. Or say, "Well, I arranged the foursome you wanted. I invited Jim, Marvin, Paul and Bill."

3. Pack a kid in his golf bag.

4. Say, "On the way home, would you pick up the two gallons of paint I've got ordered for the living room."

Fishing

1. Tell him you aren't going to keep showing his photograph to the kids, and ask him if he wants you to call him the first night they stop saying, "God bless Daddy."

2. Tell him your mother will have to come.

3. Remind him of his responsibility to Civil Defense if a disaster should occur at home while he's gone.

Unless he's like Fang, who sits on my lap during a thunderstorm, he probably won't be scared out because of your bad weather predictions.

Poker

1. As he is leaving, say, "Have fun. And if you win we'll get cough medicine for Barbie."

2. Say, "Don't hurry home. No matter how late it is, I'll be waiting up for you."

3. If you want a little extra attention, say, "Are you going to be using the .22 tonight?"

4. Ask him to fill the liquor cabinet before he goes.

And May The Best Man Emerge Victorious

1. Insist that your husband have regular checkups. It's much more enjoyable to fight with a mate in perfect health.

2. Fights should be carefully scheduled so as not to interfere with your favorite TV show or interrupt dinner hour at the police station.

3. No wound should be inflicted that cannot be covered by a standard size band-aid.

4. Nothing should be thrown that is bigger than a bread box. Have a few weapons handy but pie throwing is out of the question. Not only is it trite but, if you bake like I do, a direct hit with one of those things could kill you.

5. Remember, blood is not only thicker than water, it's much more difficult to get off the carpet.

Naturally these suggestions should be observed more strictly if you do not have a major medical insurance policy.

CHAPTER IV

The Power
Behind
The Thrown

L* A* Z* Y*

One job is enough for most men. Don't expect your husband to moonlight. Fang doesn't even sunlight. The first time he held a job for a year he expected a ticker tape parade. And he has the nerve to celebrate Labor Day. Once he lost his job and he insisted we go out and celebrate. We went from a night on the town to a year on the county. You'd do well to show concern if you find that your husband . . .

1. Fills out a personal data sheet for a job and lists all his faults.

2. Starts to picket if a factory offers to give him a job.

3. Claims he's handicapped because he's able to work.

4. Buys himself an electric thumb twiddler.

5. Has a watch that tells how many days till his retirement.

6. Counts calories not because he wants to lose weight but because he doesn't want to have any excess energy.

7. Has an electric eye in the hall that turns down the covers before he gets into the bedroom.

Even if opportunity knocks, it better be pretty darn loud or Fang won't wake up.

Behind Every Successful Man

I'm sorry to say there isn't any scientific law that covers a husband, like what lies down must get up. Fang's the only man I know with a special mattress and pillow for his work bench. Once I asked him to do something about the smell of gas and he opened a bottle of Airwick.

When he proposed he said, "We'll make such beautiful music together," but in this duet, his part seems to be all rests.

I don't mind Fang liking spectator sports, but he also likes spectator jobs.

I could tell that Fang wasn't doing well when . . .

1. He was named "Unemployed Man of the Year."

2. Five years after we were married, Fang was still paying on the license.

3. I discovered that he has an interviewer at the State Employment Office who handles only him.

4. Fang asked me to go on a business trip with him and I found out he meant going to collect our welfare check.

Everybody knows how lazy he is. One day the neighbors saw Fang mow the lawn and I got three Get Well cards.

Naturally you won't be foolish enough to expect help from your husband around the house. One day I was hanging a storm window and asked Fang if he'd give me a hand. He said, "Sure!" and started clapping. Here are a few tips which may be of value to you:

1. Save all the hard jobs for when your husband is home. You may as well have *him* watch *you* instead of only the canary.

2. If he lies on the davenport all day, maybe it would help for you to think of him as less of a husband and more of an afghan.

3. Have him ask for an outright raise and not suggest the company give merit pay. Once Fang worked where they had the merit pay system, and after six months they told him he owed the company money.

4. Don't spend a lot of money on vitamins and pep pills for your husband. Once Fang took pep pills and they worked—the only time he ever ran to bed.

5. Do everything you can to let your husband know
   you're with him. One year I was room mother at the
   unemployment office.

Helping The Helpless

If he ever gets a job and the boss invites you for dinner, here are a few tips that may help his career:

1. Do not wipe your feet as you leave their house.

2. If you break a fork on the mashed potatoes, don't make a scene—just switch to another fork or use your knife and try to slice them.

3. If the hostess says, "Come and get it!" don't yell, "Last!"

4. If the hostess asks you to have another cup of coffee, don't say, "No, thank you, I'm driving." Take the cream and sugar before, not after, you've tasted the coffee.

5. If you were invited with your children and one of the kids says, "May I please be excused?"—don't say, "Why? You didn't cook it!"

6. Above all; *DO NOT CLOSE YOUR EYES WHILE EATING.*

CHAPTER V

My Mother-In-Law Wears Army Shoes

Mothers-In-Law Do Not Make Good House Pets

Once I had the most wonderful dream—I dreamed mothers-in-law cost money and I couldn't afford one. At World Fairs they never show what a mother-in-law will be like in the year 2000, so evidently there isn't any great improvement scheduled.

It takes a lot of work and gushiness to make friends with your mother-in-law. They rarely come pre-sweetened. Expect her to be always snooping, correcting, and trying to prove you're an "under-achiever." Here are a few suggestions that may help in your relationship:

1. Do not question the age she gave you, even if it makes her only five years old when your husband was born.

2. Tell her you know her mustard plaster really helped and the penicillin the doctor sent over never would have done a thing.

3. Even though you're tempted to do so, don't read the Bill of Rights to her every time she comes over.

4. If you're trying to be syrupy sweet and your mother-in-law is the size of Moby Dick, try to remember not to say, "And how are we today?"

The Inspector General

My mother-in-law must be the probation officer I got for the crime I committed of marrying my husband.

I'm surprised she isn't nicer to me. With the kind of husband her son made, you'd think she'd be afraid I'd sue her.

Every mother thinks her son is Cary Grant, and she will never believe for a minute that by being married to her son you're going through life Tourist Class. A mother-in-law always thinks of her child first and foremost. Here is an example of what I mean. A friend of mine had her baby on the way to the hospital, and the comment of her mother-in-law was, "Everything happens to George."

All mothers-in-law have a disgusting habit . . . they come to visit you.

Discount the idea of an anonymous phone call warning yours to stay away from her son's house. Try to remember, a mother-in-law doesn't need a search warrant. Every mother-in-law has phenomenal eyesight.

From across the room she'll spot the olive pits in your garbage and know you've been drinking. Take the following precautions:

1. If you draw a caricature of your mother-in-law on the family blackboard, don't forget to erase it before she comes over.

2. Have an old pair of white gloves she slips on when she comes over to run along the furniture looking for dust so she won't have to ruin her good ones.

3. If you have a house like mine, send her upstairs to get something. There's a good chance she'll get lost.

4. No matter how tempted you are to do so, never salute her.

5. Be sure your mother-in-law has left the house for good before spraying with the air freshener.

Don't Call Us, We'll Call You

Mothers-in-law love to talk and talk and talk on the telephone. Here are some things to say to get her to hang up after she's been on the phone an hour:

1. "Oh, there's the doorbell." This is not a lie, you are not saying the doorbell is ringing.

2. "Oh, Janet, please don't drip blood on the rug."

3. "My husband's coin collection is in that desk drawer."

4. Another statement to make so your mother-in-law will get the hint and hang up: "Stop hitting Daddy so hard with the butcher knife."

The Mother-In-Law—Wife's Natural Enemy

Try not to be too obvious in your feelings about your mother-in-law. For example, don't invite her over every time there are hazardous driving warnings out.

My mother-in-law would have made a great minute man. She's always ready to fight. There may be times when you decide to escalate the war between yourself and your mother-in-law. It is unlikely that she will let the following remarks pass unnoticed:

1. "Would you consider modeling that dress in our style show? We're showing fashions of other eras."

2. "When I want your suggestions I'll put a box on the wall and you can drop them in."

3. "What Senate subcommittee are you investigating for?"

4. "We think if we scrimped a little we could present you with a trip to Siberia."

Meals Like Mother Used To Make

Drop by her house occasionally, running in with an apron on. This will make her think you're terribly busy getting meals for her son and grandchildren. Never expect a mother-in-law to give you any credit. One evening Fang said to his mother, "Phyllis put on a delicious meal tonight," and she said, "Phyllis who?"

1. Spend time on the meals you invite her to—even though it seems you should be able to just throw a fish into her mouth.

2. Learn not to be touchy about things she says. For example, don't wince if she says, "I can't understand how Harvey had ten favorite dishes when he married you, and now hasn't got one."

3. To stop your mother-in-law from insisting that you should serve her something made from scratch—serve her something you made from scratch.

Darling, Mother's Coming Home To Us

If you want your mother to come and stay with you a while—you know he's not going to pull anything with her around—here are a few arguments to present:

1. It gives you more practice in saying "Yes" so you'll do better at work.

2. Instead of taking off for a spiritual retreat you can find out about your moral inadequacies at home. She'll be like a live-in retreat master.

3. You'll save money by not going out and playing poker.

4. We'll find out what we've been doing wrong in raising the kids.

5. It'll be somebody to use all that mineral oil that you bought at a 1¢ sale.

CHAPTER VI

His Car
Has More Insurance
Than I Do

The Life You Save

Most husbands think more of their cars than of their wives. In order to have a good excuse when you wreck the family car, have your husband teach you how to drive. You can use the money you saved by not taking the Driver Education Course to take out dents.

1. When you pray for a safe trip, don't take your hands off the wheel to fold them.

2. If you have trouble remembering how to leave a car when you park on a hill, do like I did—get yourself an anchor.

3. Don't take the mirror down in the car just because it's unflattering.

4. When you're reading the road map, don't tell your husband to stay on that highway for another inch and a half.

5. Carry an oar when you drive. Three times I've ended up in water.

6. Have the man at the station put the air in the tires. I did it once myself. Have you ever seen a car with a limp?

7. Drive in heavy traffic. You aren't noticed quite as much.

8. When you don't drive very often you lose confidence —and tail lights and fenders.

9. Never become involved in a hit-and-run accident. You can't believe how depressing 25 different descriptions of yourself, all unflattering, can be.

10. Remember, only a policeman is allowed to express himself on an expressway.

Advice From A Front Seat Driver

Never let the conversation get around to your driving. Most husbands are too well prepared for you to argue the point. Even Fang has the advantage of me in this area.

1. *Phyllis:* I've already passed my driver's test. What more do you want?
   Fang: A sanity hearing.

2. *Phyllis:* I'm afraid I'm just a Sunday driver.
   Fang: No wonder so many people go to church.

3. *Phyllis:* That man damaged my car so badly it will be weeks before I can drive it.
   Fang: He'll no doubt get a safety award.

4. *Phyllis:* Is it true the safest place during a storm is in a car?
   Fang: Not when you're driving.

5. *Fang:* You're driving too fast for conditions.
   Phyllis: What conditions?
   Fang: You behind the wheel.

Just in case he's rude enough to bring up the subject, you might as well have one response handy.

6. *Fang:* Do you know *anything* about this cloverleaf?
   Phyllis: Well, I know it isn't a four-leaf cloverleaf because I never had worse luck in my life.

Officer, I Could Swear His Tail Light Turned Green

I'll never forget the cop who came up to me and said, "What gear did you have it in, Crash?" Don't try explanations like: "Well, Officer, I'll tell you — three sheep ran across in front of me, I counted them and fell asleep," or "Just like a man—you don't care about all the stop signs I *have* stopped for."

The following conversations are just a waste of time, or worse.

1. *Phyllis:* But, Officer, I've had loads of experience— 150 hours in driving tests alone. You're wasting the taxpayers' money by not passing me. I could be out paying fines.

2. *Policeman:* I don't like the way you went through that red light.
   Phyllis: Well, there's only one way to do it—fast.

3. *Phyllis:* (After hitting big truck) No use crying over spilled milk.
   Policeman: 2,000 gallons of it.

4. *Phyllis:* All I did was pass that checker cab.
   Policeman: I'm afraid I'll have to ticket you on a charge of bad checker passing.

5. *Policeman:* The driver that hit you said he didn't notice you coming.
   Phyllis: Didn't notice me? How could he miss me? I was the only car entering through an exit.

Appendix I

THE SOMETHING BORROWED IS THE TIME THEY'RE LIVING ON

An Appendix For Brides Old Enough To Know Better

If you're at the Medicare Plus One stage when you get married, urge him to splurge on your wedding gift instead of waiting for anniversaries.

Remember a nylon net veil has no warmth. You better wear your shawl also.

1. At the reception the bride should provide the Stephen Foster records.

2. You should, of course, hold your reception on the ground floor.

3. Have something for the bride to rest her hand on, as the groom slips on the ring. One ceremony I was at was held up half an hour because of shaky hands.

4. The bridegroom provides the geraniums for the altar.

5. A bride over 80 should never carry lilies. If she does she should be careful to keep her eyes open during the ceremony.

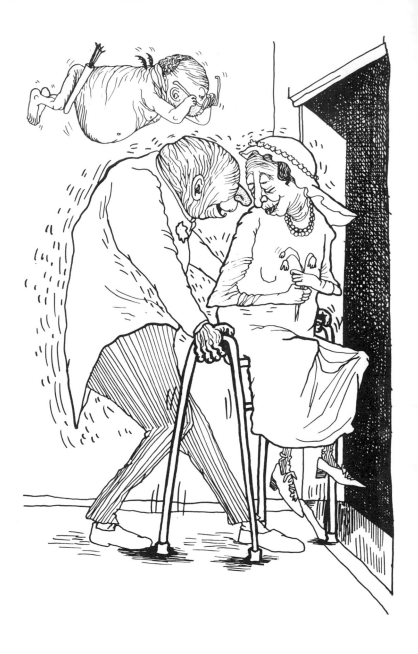

6. Have a large wedding party so in case the groom doesn't make it, he won't be missed.

7. It's all right to serve champagne at the wedding breakfast, if you're sure none of your guests are pushing their own wheel chairs.

8. If you are going across the country on your honeymoon, you had better jet. I had two friends in their nineties who were driving from New York to California. After their wedding trip I had the feeling their write-up should have read, "Mr. & Mrs. Jones will be at home in Forest Lawn."

9. If you are both 95, I would advise you not to wait eight months to get married, no matter how much the bride has her heart set on a June wedding.

10. I have not heard of a double-seated wheel chair, but perhaps you could have one specially made.

Note To Husbands:

1. Even though you can't carry her across the threshold, I'm sure your bride will appreciate being hoisted on the front of your walker as you enter your new home.

2. Twin beds are purely optional, but it's a little too much togetherness to share the same cup for your dentures.

Appendix II

THEY'RE BUILDING THEIR NEST OUT OF PLAY-DOUGH

An Appendix For Brides Young Enough To Still Have One

When you hire a person to plan your wedding, this does not include securing the groom. Plan to get married on Friday the 13th. In years to come this will make it much easier to explain why things turned out badly.

To look beautiful at your wedding, take time to plan it. It took me a long time to find two ugly bridesmaids and a frumpy little flower girl.

You are ready to get married. He still has that dollar in the bank the cleaning establishment gave him when he was born, plus 18 years of interest and 25 LP record albums. You're going to keep the baby-sitting jobs you have.

I'm sure the next edition of Child Craft will have the proper form for weddings, but until then I have some pointers that may help out in carrying off teen-age marriages successfully.

1. The bridegroom provides the rehearsal dinner the night before the ceremony. In other words, he pays for the pizzas.

2. Instruct the ushers to be careful not to offer their arms to males since sex is hard to determine.

3. Invitations are issued by the bride and not over the groom's family telephone.

4. The bridegroom provides the marriage license—or at least a down payment on it.

5. The bridegroom provides the transportation. *Do not* use the bride's Honda.

6. The bride's parents provide the Beatle records for the reception.

7. Be sure to have a large punch bowl for the chip dip.

8. It is poor taste to have cheer-leading at a wedding.

9. The groom provides the bride's ring and the bride provides the groom's. Class rings should not be used.

10. If it's a formal wedding the guests should wear *white* leather jackets.

Now about something old, something new, something borrowed, something blue. I recently went to a teen-age wedding and this is what the bride used:

Something old . . . her parents. Nothing could be considered older than her parents.

Something new . . . her ID card.

Something borrowed . . . the hub caps on the honeymoon car were "borrowed."

Something blue . . . her underwear from the one time she did the family wash.

But most important of all in young marriages, the bride should let the groom know right from the start that she is going to wear the blue jeans in the family.

Appendix III

PHYLLIS DILLER'S TEST TO DISCOVER IF YOU'RE HAPPILY MARRIED

Give yourself 10 points for every "B" checked and no points for every "A."

1. a_____You go into the bedroom and slam the door when your husband points out your domestic inadequacies.

   b_____You say, "Darling, I'm terribly interested in hearing how messy the house is, but I have a beastly headache and must go lie down. But you remember every word you were going to say and tell me later."

2. a_____You ask your husband to shovel the snow.

   b_____You say, "Only 6½ more weeks until spring. Why don't you wait, Honey?"

3. a_____You demand a personal allowance.

   b_____You assure him you are happy with what you
   get with green stamps.

4. a_____You tell him, "You've told that yarn 500
   times."

   b_____You say, "The way you tell things, George,
   that story is more delightful than the first
   time I heard it."

5. a____When you're out visiting friends and he holds out his arms showing his fish, you skeptically say, "How big?"

   b____You look at how far apart he's holding his hands and say, "That fish looked a lot bigger than that to *me*, George."

6. a____You point out the inaccuracies in the story of the deal he made when buying the car.

   b____When he tells how he conned the used car dealer you say, "George, you were even shrewder than that with him. You're always understating things."

7. a——You bawl him out on the way home from the party for the wisecrack he made about you.

b——On the way home you tell him, "I thought I'd die laughing when, after I said, 'When I lie on the beach I always burn,' you said, 'Who wouldn't with the insults you get?' I never mind when you insult me because you always do it in such a clever way."

8. a——You yawn and groan when your husband discusses football and refer to him as "That dumb athletic supporter."

b——You tell your friends, "George always knows just the play that would have made the difference in the game," and then encourage him to tell them about it.

9. a＿＿You say, "Aren't we ever going any place? If I sit home and look at these four walls another night, I'll scream."

b＿＿You say, "If there's anything I enjoy in the evening it's getting out of the kitchen and going into the living room. Every night I notice something different about this room I haven't noticed before."

10. a＿＿You call him a cheapskate when he goes over the checkbook and complains.

b＿＿You say to him, "I *like* to know when I overspend, and I think your proposed budget is just great."

PLEASE TURN OVER FOR

THE DILLER MARRIAGE

TEST SCORE CARD

	A.	B.
1.		
2.		
3.		
4.		
5.		
6.		
7.		
8.		
9.		
10.		

Add _____ _ _ _ _ _ _ _ _ _

SCORE

If you scored between 100 and 70—you're incredibly stupid. Ask your family to institutionalize you.

If you scored between 70 and 40—some people never learn. You appear to be one of them.

If you scored between 40 and 10—the honeymoon is over. Congratulations.